Zoom in on
DOMESTIC ROBOTS

Jill Sherman

E | **Enslow Publishing**
101 W. 23rd Street
Suite 240
New York, NY 10011
USA

enslow.com

WORDS TO KNOW

artificial intelligence Software that allows a computer to reason and learn.

computer A programmable machine.

invent To make something new.

machine A device that people operate.

program A set of computer instructions.

robot A programmable device that does tasks automatically.

sensor A part of a robot that helps it understand the world around it.

technology Tools, machines, or processes for human needs.

CONTENTS

Every day we get a little closer to a world with robot helpers.

Robots in Your Home

Wake up! Your robot bed is your new alarm. It rolls you out from the covers. Sleepy, you walk to the kitchen. What do you want to eat? Eggs? Toast? Cereal? You press a button. A robot arm readies your breakfast.

Get Ready

Now, it's time to get ready. You enter the bathroom. You press the button labeled "school." Robot arms fly toward you. They

Robots can do tasks that some people find boring.

brush your teeth. They comb your hair. They bring you fresh clothes.

How would you like to live in this world? One day soon, robots may be doing all kinds of chores for us.

Task Masters

We use robots for jobs that are hard or boring. Robots can do many tasks. Some clean your floors. Others feed your pets.

But we already use machines to do many daily tasks. How are robots any different? A robot is still

Long Ago

People have imagined mechanical robots since ancient times. Famous artist Leonardo da Vinci even imagined a world with robots. He drew up plans for one in 1495.

Light sensors help robots understand the world around them.

a machine. But robots "know" what they are doing. You do not need to operate a robot. Set the robot to work. Then walk away. The robot does not need your help. It already knows its task.

Plus, robots can sense the world around them. You have five senses. They are sight, sound, smell, taste, and touch. Robots need senses, too. That is why they have sensors.

Building a Robot

Nobody likes chores. Why not put a robot to the task? So, scientists invented the robot vacuum. But making a robot that works takes time. Many pieces have to work together. They have to run without you there. If the robot can't work on its own, it's not much of a robot!

Robot vacuums roam your floors, cleaning up while you relax.

Robot Vacuum

When scientists made the robot vacuum, they gave it a body. Not a body like yours. Not even one like a normal vacuum cleaner. They gave it a body good for its task: cleaning the floor. The robot would not need a person to operate it. So the robot did not need a long handle. It would have to reach under furniture. So it had to be low to the ground. A robot also needs to move. So scientists gave it wheels.

10

People write programs that give robots their instructions.

Sensors

Remember that robots need to sense the world. The robot vacuum has sensors. They are along its edge. The robot rolls along the floor. Soon it hits a wall. The sensor knows. It sends a message to the robot's computer.

The computer is the robot's "brain." Scientists filled the computer with instructions. The instructions are called a program. The program tells the robot what to do.

When the sensor feels the wall, it tells the computer. The program tells the robot to change direction. This happens again and again. Soon the robot has cleaned the entire room!

First Robot

George Devol built the first robot, the Unimate. General Motors put the Unimate to work. It began assembling cars in 1961.

Robot, Do My Chores!

Mop the floor. Mow the lawn. Feed the dog. Water the plants. The chores never end. Now you know that robots can lighten the load. So, are you ready for a robot of your own?

Scrub and Mow

One of the most popular robots is the robot vacuum. But this design has gotten some upgrades. Similar robots can help with other chores. No more mopping the floor! Scientists redesigned the robot. They put cleaning pads on the bottom. Now, it can scrub the kitchen floor.

A bigger bot has room for mower blades. Set up an invisible fence. The sensors can tell where the lawn ends. No more mowing the lawn!

Don't Forget the Pets

This robot can cut the grass!

We love our pets. Make sure they never miss a meal. A robotic pet feeder will do the trick. The device senses when your pet's bowl is empty. It opens a door and fresh food or water floods into the bowl.

What goes in must come out. Cleaning up after your cat can be tough. Not with a robotic litter box! The bot senses when your cat has visited. After, it sifts the waste. It goes into a sealed drawer. Now kitty always has fresh litter

No More Snoozing

Set your alarm clock. In the morning it beeps. You hit the snooze. A few minutes later it beeps again. Snooze. Before you know it, you're late for school.

Pet Pals

When you're away, your pet can play! New devices let pet owners keep in touch with their furry friends all day. With Pawley or Rovio, you can watch, talk to, and even play with your pet. Though not a true robot (yet!), it is a great way to keep pets happy.

A robot can help cook, too. This robot is sprinkling cheese on a pizza.

Need an extra nudge? Try a robot alarm. When you go to hit the snooze, Clocky rolls away! You may try to stay in bed. But the blare of the alarm gets louder. It zips around the room. There's only one way to stop the noise. You have no choice. Get out of bed and chase it down. Time to start the day!

Your Robotic Future

What would you like a robot to do for you? With the proper design, the sky is the limit. Scientists are dreaming up new robots, too.

Robotic Cars and Butlers

Need a ride to school? Robots may soon supply the ride. Many companies are building cars that drive themselves. The cars

Driverless cars are already being tested by companies like Google.

are covered in sensors. They can see the street and cars around them. To get to school, the car would follow a map. Just like a GPS!

Robot butlers are also coming soon. The robot would follow you around your home. It could answer your questions, bring you snacks, and play music. Life with robots sounds like fun.

The Future of Robots

It may be a long time before robots can do ALL our chores. But every day, scientists are improving robots. Hundreds of new robots are in the making.

Most robots do just one task. And people do many things better than

Price Tags

Robotic technology does not come cheap. Many robot vacuums cost five hundred dollars or more. The more advanced the technology, the more expensive the robot.

Keep in mind the tasks your robot needs to complete when you create its design.

robots. You can pick up a pencil, a water glass, or a bowling ball. Robots have a hard time with this. Say the robot picks up the glass. But it only knows how to pick up bowling balls. The glass will shatter!

It's hard for robots to learn new skills. Scientists designed artificial intelligence. It is software for the robot. It helps the robot reason and learn. Still, few robots can mimic human conversation. Scientists are trying to solve these problems.

One day, robots could be taking care of all our household chores!

21

ACTIVITY:
NO MORE CHORES!

What is your least favorite chore? Is there a way a robot could help?
Design a robot helper.

What you'll need:

paper
pencils, markers, or crayons

How to make it:

1. Pick one task, like picking up toys or loading the dishwasher.

2. What does the robot need to do? Does it need arms? Wheels? Draw a robot body. Design it so that it can move the way it needs to.

3. How will the robot sense its world? Will it sense light? Sound? Can it feel the walls? Place sensors on your robot and label them.

4. Now write a set of instructions. What will it do when it turns on? How will it know to do something new? What happens next? How will your robot know when its job is done?

5. You have all the basics ready. Share your idea with friends. Maybe you can build a beginner model of your idea!

LEARN MORE

Books

Stewart, Melissa. *National Geographic Readers: Robots.* New York, NY: National Geographic Children's Books. 2014.

Tuchman, Gail. *Robots*. New York, NY: Scholastic. 2015.

Zuchora-Walske, Christine. *Robots at Home*. Minneapolis, MN: Lerner Books. 2014.

Websites

Galileo Educational Network: Robotics
galileo.org/robotics
Engaging students in science and engineering by giving them the tools to invent and build using digital technology.

Idaho Public Television Diaglogue for Kids: Robots
idahoptv.org/sciencetrek/topics/robots
Watch helpful videos showing how robots are used everywhere, from work to home.

INDEX

Published in 2018 by Enslow Publishing, LLC.
101 W. 23rd Street, Suite 240, New York, NY 10011

Library of Congress Cataloging-in-Publication Data

Names: Sherman, Jill, author.
Title: Zoom in on domestic robots / Jill Sherman.
Description: New York : Enslow Publishing, [2018] | Series: Zoom in on robots | Includes bibliographical references and index.
Identifiers: LCCN 2017021490| ISBN 9780766092310 (library bound) | ISBN 9780766094444 (pbk.) | ISBN 9780766094451 (6 pack)
Subjects: LCSH: Personal robotics—Juvenile literature. | Robots—Juvenile literature. | Robotics—Juvenile literature. | Human-robot interaction—Juvenile literature.
Classification: LCC TJ211.416 .S54 2018 | DDC 629.8/92—dc23
LC record available at https://lccn.loc.gov/2017021490

Printed in the United States of America

Photos Credits: Cover, p. 1 Andrey_Popov/Shutterstock.com; p. 4 David Mcnew/AFP/Getty Images; p. 6 Frank Perry/AFP/Getty Images; p. 8 zorazhuang/iStockphoto.com; p. 10 Kyodo News/Getty Images; p. 11 izusek/iStockphoto.com; p. 14 Jaap Arriens/NurPhoto/Getty Images; p. 16 Ingo Wagner/DPA/Getty Images; p. 18 Kim Kulish/Corbis News/Getty Images; p. 20 Georgijevic/iStockphoto.com; p. 21 Yoshikazu Tsuno/AFP/Getty Images; p. 22 Darrin Henry/Shutterstock.com; graphic elements cover, p. 1 (background) Perzeus/Shutterstock.com; pp. 2, 3, 22, 23 sketchvector/Shutterstock.com; pp. 5, 9, 13, 17 Macrovector/Shutterstock.com; pp. 8, 10, 12, 14, 16 all_is_magic/Shutterstock.com.